A Fire of Prayer

*A Collection of
Poetry and Photography*

Gina Marselle

Praise for the Author

"In *A Fire of Prayer*, poetry and photographic images compliment each other perfectly. No illustration here, but each genre strong and true. Marselle's images sometimes make me think of Margaret Bourke-White's great industrial photographs. Sometimes they meet the eye more softly and organically. Her poems are the same, drawing on the many different situations and emotions of life to say their piece with unique originality."

~Margaret Randall
author of *Ruins* and *Daughter of Lady Jaguar Shark*

"*A Fire of Prayer* is an exquisite and powerful collection of poems and photographs. Startling in their manner to coax the vulnerable and the sacred, they are poem-prayers for happiness. Safety. Love. Peaceful times. Crafted by a mother's tendered tribute to life, they swell, bloom, and nurture. They resuscitate, resurrect, revive. Marselle strums loneliness as a new verse and we hum along."

~Levi Romero, author of *A Poetry of Remembrance* and
Sagrado: A Photopoetics Across the Chicano Homeland

"Light has never been so affectionate—or so welcoming of the shadows that bend our lives generation upon generation. The combination of Gina Marselle's photography and poetry offers definitions of both gravity and compassion, an interplay inviting the witness to simply *hush* and be present. *A Fire of Prayer* merits the risk all openings (even pages) entail. Upon finishing the last syllable on the last page, each reader becomes part of a collective who can say—and truly mean it: "Into the light we stared."

~Lisa Gill
author of *Dark Enough* & *The Relenting*

Copyright © 2015 Swimming with Elephants Publications
First Edition

All rights reserved. No portion of this publication may be reproduced, stored in a retrieval system, or transmitted in any form or by any other means, electronic, mechanical, photocopying, or recording without prior permission of Gina Marselle unless such copying is expressly permitted by federal copyright law. Address inquiries in permissions to: Swimming with Elephants Publications: swimmingwithelephants.com

All Photography, including cover photography, copyright © Gina Marselle - all rights reserved.

Contents

Dig, Sophia, Dig 9
Melancholy 13
What If— 14
Skeleton Bones 15
Substance 17
on days like this, ... 21
Time Traveler 25
Defining Spirituality 29
Woody Woodpecker Remnants 35
But I Don't Write Like Neruda 38
A Mother's Body 41
Mīror 44
Ode to My Son 45
tangerine 49
Life 51
Heading North 55

About the Author 58
Acknowledgements 61
Gratitude 61

Part I

~

Finding Breath

Dig, Sophia, Dig

> *"...if my life is like the dust*
> *that hides the glow of the rose*
> *what good am I*
> *Heaven only knows..."*
>
> ~Clyde Otis

rhythm and blues
    pour through speakers
        as Dinah sings
            fragmented tones

shattering the quiet
    unearthing burden
        dig, Sophia, dig
            share your wisdom

personified
    in biblical verse
        hidden in lines
            of King Solomon's song

feel *This Bitter Earth*
    quake when my voice cries
        as the potter builds
            my body's architecture

from soft clay
    her hands dancing like music
        shaping eyes, nose, mouth
            heart, belly, pelvis, toes

like my lover knows
    the outline of my body
        the inline of my soul
            Sophia fills—

a potter's touch
    molding life,
        affection, compassion
            wrapping water

like a silk web
    wraps a housefly
        for garden spider's consumption,
            a natural design

throwing and throwing me
    on the wheel, I drown in this
        wrapping of water,
            suffocating, calming—

breathe the water
    resuscitate, resurrect, revive
        dig, Sophia, dig
            empty this pain

fill us each with love
    instead of empty with wants
        make us whole again
            lure your wisdom

from the recess of your labyrinth
    soothe fears, anxieties, uncertainty
        this world dances with the devil,
            we've forgotten

to hold him at bay with harmony
        the news riddles day to day mirth
                my children will suffer
                        if this bitter earth

doesn't repair, repair, repair—
        the potter places me in the kiln
                I corrode inflexible
                      prepare for a life of

suffering, so I may survive
        teach children to survive,
                Wisdom scripts upon the
                      snowy belly of dove
truth,
        beauty,
                love,
                      peace

Sophia's still digging, digging, digging,
unearthing letter by letter—

h
        o
                p
                        e

dig, Sophia, dig
hollow hope from bitter earth—

Melancholy

The black stones of loss
sow dark-cloud sky.

Desolate heartbeats
count the deserted

black and blue pulses
of the D chord.

She strums loneliness,
as a new verse.

Gathers odes
and love poems

to burn each
into ghostly smoke,

staining
phantom clouds gray.

What If—

What if
there is no beginning
or end?

What if
time doesn't exist
and this dejected sky swallows the fiery sun?

What if
each moment is covered
with snowflakes and ash?

What if
each is a forgotten prayer
or unknown song?

What if
psalms form rhymes
without sounds?

What if our whispers
leave echoes scattered in silence
        emptied upon an
                unpaved
                        world?

What if
our skin is wrapping paper
unwrapping scars intertwining us together?

Will we still hurt?

Skeleton Bones

Her loneliness wraps
like skeleton bones

tying pretty little red bows
in make believe.

Swans dance on stage,
and daffodils sing folksy songs.

Rolling out high notes
about climbing mountaintops

to see the breath of God
dissipating thunderclouds.

Substance

"The years that are gone seem like dreams—if one might go on sleeping and dreaming—but to wake up and find—oh! well! Perhaps it is better to wake up after all, even to suffer, rather than to remain a dupe to illusions all one's life."

~Kate Chopin

I read the news insatiably.
I'm like an army of black ants
devouring giant sunflowers
when it comes to headlines.
My husband tells me I have an answer
for everything from nuclear science
to cracking an egg.

It's because I read *npr* news, *mayoclinic.org*,
The Huffington Post, *The New York Times*,
National Geographic, even *Horse&Rider*.

I send articles to my mom,
friends, teachers, my daughter.
I devour poetry books, revel in articles
about what your toddler's thinking or
devouring.

But,
sometimes,
the news is too much,
and stories play inside-out
inside my head—

Today, I read a story:
A Mother, 42, Commits Suicide

the headline bellows.
She's a politician's wife.
I can't remember their names.
The number 42 captures my attention.
The sharp edges of 4,
the sloping line of 2
Sadness tightens.

I remember my Uncle David
who committed suicide in '07,
after years of depression and addiction.

I can hear his laughter.

My husband still mourns his best friend Boltz
who took his own life,
leaving so many behind—
most importantly his baby daughter.

We listen to his recorded
alternative rock songs and weep.

My cousin Joseph, battling cancer,
ended his life in '13 to ease his pain.
His obit reads:
He loved camping, his wife, kids—

my grandpa's voice catches when he talks
about Joe.

Sad smiles that hide hopelessness—
all gone too soon.

When I read stories about suicide,
my breath pauses as this woman's death weeps.
I feel for her children, her husband.

There's a black and white snapshot
beneath the bellowing headline—
sitting in a row are her three kids,
her balding husband,
and the family's dejected black lab.
As I read the article,
I wonder, did she sit silent
inside some kind of madness.
Her loneliness, too much,
the world's space, too much.
Sitting inside the noise of her children,
too much.

She died alone.
A gruesome death,
slitting her own throat.

What did her husband feel when he found her
latent on the floor. Cold. Heart broken, bleeding
like butterfly wings flap carrying the blue sky
across the round shape of earth.

When I'm 42,
I'll be a mother of a rambunctious toddler,
teenage daughter, a wife
teacher, writer,
crazy for life.
I'll live that year
in memory of the year hope got lost.
I'll remember the
moment I read about her
in the moments
my kids are too
loud,
I'll tell myself,
Hush,

that is beauty.
When my husband frustrates me,
I'll say,
Hush,
that is your heartbeat.
When the stories in the news
are to ugly to fathom reality,
I'll say,
Hush,
let's capture life and fit it into shapes.

I'll say a prayer,
find my breath in thanksgiving,
love all the geometric spaces
fill each with wonder.

When I'm 42,
I'll live, make changes.
Inspire. Teach.
In moments of sadness,
I'll not live in misconceptions.
This is my life given.

It is better to wake up after all,
even to suffer, rather than to
remain a dupe to illusions
all one's life.

I wish I could have shared that
in the twinkling before she died.

on days like this,

       my bone china teacup is full,
brimming with hot water
and organic loose-leaf peppermint tea.

       I wrap small hands
around its warmth,
hold firm,

as if someone who cares
is holding my hand.

       sanctuary
is felt
as the tea's aroma
arouses sleepy senses.
my thoughts, anxieties
are company.
early morning birds sing
before the light of sun rise,
the dog cozy by feet,
family sleeps.

       I read an article
on the science of loneliness.
it is titled "Death by Loneliness"
the byline is anonymous.
this candid article is about his mother,
who passed away
at only 49.
one line from
the literature
jumps out
desperate for attention:

"I think my mother died of loneliness.
that wasn't on her death certificate,
but she had all the symptoms…
loneliness swallowed her at times…."

       as a kid, I use to throw
rocks into the well
at my grandparent's 100 year old farmhouse
in Port Byron, IL.
the rocks would fall deep,
deeper
into the black shadow of nothingness.
after some time,
a gentle, muffled
splash
filtered up empty.
even as a child, I knew what it must be like
to be swallowed up by loneliness.

       this article is remarkably dismal,
about depression,
human nature,
is by nature
social,
so why are so many isolated?
attacked by that deep
endorphin-destroying monster
of imbalance,
too weak to see
truth
or balance worth.

   on days like this,
life offers
little
for
tomorrow's
sun.

   I don't care who you are,
loneliness
like depression
lives
in doses
of imbalance,
and sometimes
it is worse than just depression
like the billowing gray cloud waves
rushing over the sandias,
as if the world is being swallowed
by a monotonous universe.

   my teacup is half full,
still warm.
I wrap my hands around,
hold firm.
warmth seeps into my
bones.
for a moment,

comfort is felt.

Time Traveler

*This poem is inspired by
New Mexico Artist's Cari Pier's
painting titled "Time Traveler"*

there's this one crow I see when I'm out running
or walking to the store
or looking at this painting
he cries to me
in aching sadness
I imagine his tone
throughout his travels
droning in his wing flap
gliding
like an ancient bomber hums
over summer desert winds
his paper shadow kite suspended in animation
along the mesa

he moves from the blue earth
to hours of darkness
his intuition is guided by dim stars
his stone gaze always searching
like ancient compass
never falters
his sorrow echoes
my meditative dreamscape
we meet again
I carry my paintbrush like a bronze sword
he paints his journey
from the tip of his painted feathers
to the roundness of pale moon
his oboe heart beats in melodic sobs
with the drum of earth beating in waves

find center
search for the middle path
enlightenment is found in some
lapis lazuli spectrum
I notice that the crow holds heaven
under his wing span

he survives as a scavenger
picks
tears
rips at the flesh of his own heart
he makes no qualms
he is lost
on this path
the earth's flight lines have crossed
colors are blending
everything is murky
lone crow caws
and I weep
in aching sadness
like travelers of time
my path
his flight
echoes
from blue earth
to black hour of darkness
we dance
to notes painted in depression
across landscapes
our bleeding hearts
flooding the path with sadness

now what do we do

as the crow soars into an abyss
meditation brings me to the edge
of a dream

I survive as an artist
paint
dab
brush paint across the canvas of my heart
I make no qualms
I'm lost
on this path
the earth's topography bleeds
blending pigments
until everything is murky

so I painted a path
in the center
and I walk upon it
everyday
it's getting worn
becoming familiar

there's this one crow I see when I'm out running
or walking to the store
or looking at this painting
he cries to me
in aching sadness

so I painted a path for him…

Defining Spirituality

"The LORD is my light and my salvation…"

~King James Version of Psalms 27:1

I.

Spirituality spiders
like a web of morning light.
Mindful of the day's toil.
Solitude lingers,
hollowed inside a mother robin's song.
Sacred Sun pushes Dawn's shadows aside.
Sunflower seedlings push through the dirt,
unfolding effortlessly.
Sipping piñon chocolate coffee,
weary from dreams, anxious for stillness,
calming waves of uncertainty.
It's a daily struggle
like taming the wind
after a springtime storm.
In between realms
of consciousness and unconsciousness—
This is my Easter Vigil, my lament from fear.
Desperate to let go
to define the
undefined—
making sense
of scrabble tiles
randomly pulled.
The morning's unchanging
adds structure,
predictability, eases fear.
Radio sounds buzz the day's weather,

warm, sunny—a communal cloudless,
blue day reaching all directions of the Zia—
Spirituality spiders like a web of morning light.

II.

Still the mind,
        practice the breath.

                Inhale downward dog,
                      exhale runner's lunge,

                        inhale standing mountain,
                            exhale flat back,

        inhale child's pose,
            exhale warrior one.

Inhale tree pose,
        exhale Namaste hands,

thumbs to heart
beat still alive.

Thankful in each breathe.

Still the mind.

Empty uncertainty.

Death overtures into
                headline news
                        tickers across thoughts.

Sometimes
>> the world's pain
> intertwines with consciousness—
>>> exhale fear,

inhale resolution.

Change the channel,
> still the mind.

Practice yoga,
> interlacing meditations

>> with whispering psalms—

>>> finding solace.

Part II

~

Finding Solace

Woody Woodpecker Remnants

By the time I was five,
we moved into our second home.
A big one story, ranch style house
in the Hog Capital of the world,
Kewanee, Il.
It was painted white
with black shutters.
An island house—
surrounded by a surreal green sea-lawn,
as if Andre Breton or Salvador Dali
painted it brilliant.
Trees dappled every part of the house.

The heartbeat of the house
belonged to the kitchen. The window over the sink
allowed the morning sun to flood the pristine white walls and tile
floors.
Everything was radiant. Clean.
The early spring breeze blew calm.
I sat on the floor with my baby brother coloring,
as my mom unpacked.
I colored Woody Woodpecker using sharp-pointed,
Crayola crayons. Hoping Mom would place it
on the fridge. I colored that acorn woodpecker ritzy red,
with a bright blue suit, staying in the lines
and adding shade where needed.
My baby brother cooed in his bouncer.
I watched that he didn't fuss.

Mom buzzed around in her white, skeletal jeans and a T.
Her reddish hair
bounced pass her shoulders.
She was movie star picturesque.

I watched her out of the corner of my eye as the
kitchen went from bare bones
to cozy with a "Home Sweet Home"
picture framed on the wall.

The clock's hour hands went by in warp speed.
The sun went from morning till afternoon.
With the time change so came the winds.
In the spring the Midwest weather changes
with a breath.
Thunder rolled in the background
drowning out the radio tunes of the Bee Gees.
The curtains whipped as my mom struggled to get
the kitchen window closed.
She knocked over her crystal ashtray, and it
shattered in tiny pieces as her cigarette
scattered in slow motion across the floor.
I picked up the still lit cigarette
and threw it in the sink.
By now the sky was angry gray.
The tress branches bended to the earth's floor,
as if stretching for the greenness to anchor.
The tornado sirens wailed.
My mother grabbed us and yelled for the dog.
We tripped down the stairs in a hurried fashion.
My mother hunkered down over us with her arms
spread angel-wing wide.
The earth and sky yelled and fought.
Screamed and dragged. Crunched and broke.
We laid still.
Hunched in a corner where only spiders dwell.

A minute or two later all was quiet.
Destruction tore a hole where our house once
stood. Into the light we stared.
On the corner edge of our bitten out kitchen floor

was my Woody Woodpecker coloring book
open to the page I carefully colored.
His wings spread wide
welcoming us from our shadowy hole.

But I Don't Write Like Neruda

When I sit on opposite ends of the couch
from my husband watching
reruns of *The King of Queens,*
I think about love poems I could write,
but don't.
We wrap ourselves under a blanket,
so that the winter chill
sits outside our snug warmth. Jealous.
I'm content with the laugh track
timed to the wisecracks of Doug and Carrie.
We lay cold toes on each other's lap,
quietly massaging aches.
Our feet pulse against the pressure of this kneading.
We fit nicely together.
Marriage
fills emptiness
with belonging, any kind of belonging.
Even our breath belonging.
Inhaling and exhaling as one.
With each beat,
lungful,
and melody
surviving in this world
in slim tales and lights and shadows
mirrors faced each day,
never forgetting any
history of self.
Finding similarities between ourselves
and the reruns we watch.
Sometimes we have to blanket imperfections
inside the comfort of breath,
inside a Neruda-like love poem.

But I don't write like Neruda.

So my love poems come from the
inhales and exhales of marriage
in quiet moments like this.

A Mother's Body

"Do not let this universe regret you."

~ Marty McConnell

A mother's body is a tribute to this world.
Her body endures.
Her spirit battles—
Each night she runs a piping hot bath.
Bubbled hot with lavender salts to melt away the day's disorder.
Before the mirror she studies her naked body.
It's a typography littered imperfectly.
She makes a mental list.
Flabby this.
Flabby that.
She studies her body,
moves closer to the mirror
hunts like a warrior for scars, gray hairs,
stretch marks,
cellulite,
age spots,
cancer.
Tears come
because she can't love this.

A mother's body is a tribute to this world.
She reminds herself. She scolds her negativity.
This body has given birth twice. Two times her
body held life.
She holds her fleshy breast in her aging hand.
A single drop of milk falls from nipple to belly
to the cold stone tile floor.
This is life.
This breast, fed her children.
This is beauty.

A mother's body is a tribute to this world.
Her shoulders are designed for her husband to kiss.
Melting silk white skin like a butterfly to sky
into wrinkled elbows,
into wrists and small hands.
This body birthed from her mother's womb from
grandmother's body,
from God.
Here's her troubled heart, her lonely prayers, her
worry and fears
wrapped in her empty lung,
her narrow waist,
her protruding belly that refuses flatness.
Why does this body cause her such sorrow?
She nourishes self with rich foods, salads and fruit.
Breads and meat—
It's too much sometimes. Cake and coffee adds
layers of fat.
Yoga and running isn't enough to battle against
this body. She endures. She stuffs
those pretty summer dresses in the back of her
closet to wear again,
someday.

A mother's body is a tribute to this world,
a mantra to fill her unfilled belly button—
full of laughter and honey.
Her caesarean scar is a warrior's birthing canal
into motherhood.   Down-to-earth
violin hips play a tune to soothe,
held firm with bone
undeniably full thighs
bursting from skin like an abyss—
sways with husband's dance,
rocks baby to and fro,

holds a graceful dress like an hourglass.

A mother's body is a tribute to this world.
Her strong knees, calves
and hallow ankle bone allow movement.
Her calloused feet sculpt purpose.
Her skin is tattooed in wounds, stretched strong
holding bone, blood, muscle.
Stormy eyes shaping her soul, full lips mouthing
words of wisdom,
        maybe teenage daughter will listen.

A mother's body is imperfect.
Her life
interrupted
with insecurities   her weight   her husband her job her
children her art her she I
me
overweight with love,

here's   my
        body
            naked.

Each night before my bath
I whisper,
I'm a tribute to this world.

Mīror

> *"There are two ways of spreading one's light: to be the candle or the mirror that reflects it."*
>
> ~Edith Wharton

This journey is to open heart and fill the page with poetry. Fill the page to quiet the mind. The yogi's journey touches hands with that poet's heart. The goddess of woman ages into wrinkled toes and settled hands. The stillness of her hair whispers nothingness as she folds into sacred ampleness. Elongating spine into the empty page she begins with the omega. A fire of prayer burns inside to purge worry. Worry walks like a well-sharpened knife prepared to paper-thin cut a tomato. Slicing ever so gently as to not cut self to bleed crimson as pain flows like a pink jellyfish in the Atlantic. Motherhood is painfully tiresome. Oceans of waves guide this journey from tributes to disappointments. From a cocooned voice soothing baby's tear-soaked cheeks to tying shoes to tutus to honor roll to broken hearts. The earth bares scars from daughter's knee as she falls from bike's first ride. Tippy toes from her room to sneak into mother's bed like a ballerina en pointe on a sprung floor. Soft, smooth, perfect alignment. Her dreams are quieted by mother's breath. The night's journey is to bring comfort and heal the body from the day's battle. Evening prayers bless life. Bless the day. Ease worry with rested eyes. Rested body. Warrior hearts beat in time. From the womb daughter's stubbornness matches mother's patience. Together they hold each other up, as the day can sometimes be long. The battle is strong as teenager explores independence; mother's hand caresses her newborn for preparation for the day daughter grows into her own womanhood. One day ago this tiny-being perfect beyond breath gave life to her mother's heart. Mother gave daughter the only name suited for a miracle. Mir. *Miror. Mirari. Miratus sum. Miranda.*

Ode to My Son

"We are shaped by our thoughts; we become what we think. When the mind is pure, joy follows like a shadow that never leaves."

~ Buddha

"I love the handful of earth you are."

~Pablo Neruda

Be still. Listen.
Make it all count.
Observe every sunset as a kiss from God,
every breezy day as a blessing.
Fill your papá's zapatos with your growing dedos del los pies.
He hopes you have his nose, I hope you have his strong manos
to make the ones you love feel safe.
Tell him you love him often,
"Te amo, te amo, te amo."

Let your baby voice sing.
Be as patient as the Sandias.
Laugh always,
your smiles are joyous.

Stay brave.
Be the one to help,
to keep promises.

Eres un ángel,
round cheeks,
manos gordas,
soft skin,
ticklish Buddha belly.

My son,
su Papá's Rey.
This is my ode to true love—
because when loved swelled my heart,
you swelled my womb.
Baby boy,
Kanito,
my daily prayer is that you're happy,
safe,
loved.
That our shared world seeks peaceful times.
That wishes become dreams become goals
become reality.
That you know your sister Miranda's
passion is dance.
That she dances, always.
When she holds you, when she eats, in line at Walgreens.
She pliés, jumps, stretches, and talks to you.
She loves your apple blossom cheeks,
thinks they're perfection.
That you play fútbol with su hermano, Santiago,
build tents out of old cottonwood branches.
That you know this love.

Your mother's love,
Your father's love—
protecting your newborn helplessness.
Tiny head,
eyes closed,
snoring peacefully.
Pale, smooth skin,
blue veins beneath like little rivers
flow,
seeking mouth, suckling
tongue for full breast.

Son, you sound like a warthog,
gulping down nutrients.

Growing.
Observing.

The first time your Papá swaddled you—

miracle.

The first time you closed tiny fingers around my finger—

miracle.

The world's anger we can't shield,
we can only raise you to stand tall, to have
integrity,
strength,
confidence.

Who will you become?
What word will you share first?
When will you crawl, walk, run?

Milestones logged in your baby book.
(Holding your head up, holding your bottle, eating rice cereal,
standing with aide, rolling over, pushing yourself up during tummy
time, outgrowing your bathtub, one day turns to three months to
four months to growing so mas).

Your steel-blue eyes turning
in the still world as a sage who seeks answers.
Their color
brilliant now
gray blue green brown gold
quiet earth colors.

My littlest one,
Kanito,
I named you.
Kano (\k(a)-no\) of Japanese origin,
meaning one's masculine's power, capability.
The god of water.
Nicholas for victory, patron saint of children and seafarers.
Ryuu for dragon spirit,
Rebolledo your Chilean father's last name.
Honor it well.

Be still. Listen.
Make it all count.
Observe every sunset as a kiss from God,
every breezy day as a blessing.

tangerine

a tangerine tree melts fire into sun,
illuminates ash, empties solitude
dreaming yellow ocean waves,
all the while the earth spins
i
stand still
like Maria in *Westside Story*
the scene blurs
seeing Tony across the dance floor—
love
is so rosy
accidental meeting, fate seals
the stars blend
satellites in the sky blink, love dies
tick tock, tick tock
time evaporates memories,
leaves sorrow in the color of blue lizard tongues
and gray desert fields—
i will paint
my feelings across paper
with letters forming words
dotting each i—
will paint my feelings
retire my camera, burn images,
creating—is for the inspired.

Life

Generations,
family,
time
slips by
like water between
fingers.
My infant son holds my finger
as he sleeps.
We drive to Chicago,
my Dad,
daughter,
son,
and
me—
The car zooms.
Baby snores.
Daughter reads
about horses.
I try to read
The Perks of Being a Wallflower,
but my mind wanders
as my dad drives
this drive
I have seen a thousand times
since I was 10
from Sycamore to Chicago
a mindless zoom
until we are closer to Chi town.
I envision the skyline
the same since childhood.
It's still exciting.

We're heading to Shedd's Aquarium
because daughter has memory of going there
when she was three—
then a raining day, today sunny, 72 degrees.
Cooler than Albuquerque
where husband waits
missing his infant son.
Although, I send an iPhone video
(and snapshots),
our infant son grows more these two weeks,
he gains confidence,
says "mama" when frustrated.
He has made himself at home here visiting.
His big sis always chasing after him.
He crawls faster trying to escape,
being only eight months old
he explores, discovers
bumps his head, eats Grammy's baked chicken,
makes songs on pots and pans,
tears petals from Grammy's garden while laughing.
Grammy has named him "Kano the Barbarian."
He Races his G-pa,
crawling across the living room floor,
climbing up his recliner, tackling his computer.
Baby K looks at my brother like kindred souls made for mischief,
lays his head on his shoulder content,
looks for his Dada.
Smiles his gummy, two bottom teeth grin when his Dada calls.
Living far away aches the heart.
Aches the heart to leave husband alone

with the dog.
As time slips
like water between fingers,
next Tuesday
we'll be home in Albuquerque.
There my mind will wander
explore photos remembering
Midwest home.

Heading North

Even though the winds chime
different vocabularies,
my dreams linger in stillness
as the Southwest train rocks with a constant
vibration. We're heading North toward Chicago
for my brother's wedding.
24-hour train rides sanction thinking.

The landscape changes while sleeping—
it transforms from endless desert sand
to endless cornstalks.
We pass Kansas City,
a tiresome bridge crossing
the meandering Mighty Mississippi,
into *pretty how towns*.

Each time I travel this route
I'm taken back to Mrs. Johnson's third grade class
where we recited a song
to spell the Great River correctly—

Go, Mississippi, you're on the right track,
Go, Mississippi, and this is a fact,
Go, Mississippi, you'll never look back,
M-I-S-S-I-S-S-I-P-P-I...
we always giggled at P-P,
and Mrs. Johnson always said, "Now Class..."

It seems a thousand years since moving from
Northern Illinois to Central New Mexico.
From the Land of Lincoln
to the Land of Enchantment
where the Zia flag symbolizes

the sacred number four—
the four points of the compass,
four seasons of the year,
four periods of the day,
four phases of life—

continuing, moving, forward,
racing the tracks.

This growing old frightens me.

What if time passes too quickly,
and I can't catch hold?

To me, this train ride
is sanctity. Time stands still—
I catch up with teenage daughter
about the latest book, lyric,
or *The Vampire Diaries*.
I hold Baby Boy who's not
at all willing to sit still.
Husband's first train ride,
and he doesn't see the beauty
in the rock of the sleeper,
his eldest, my step-son is content
watching *The Lego® Movie*.

We take frequent breaks,
play 21,
step off at the "smoke" stops
to stretch, twist, and
breathe deeply fresh air,
laugh at the sky.
Hop back anxiously awaiting
for the call of our station
without delay

the conductor calls out,
Mendota, IL.

Dad picks us up and asks,
"How was the train ride?"
Everyone has a complaint.

But not really.

Chicago's suburbs are
country living,
slow, lazy summers
breezy ease of livin' invented here.

On the way to Dad's,
we stop at *Steak 'n Shake* for a burger, fries,
and a delicious chocolate, hand-dipped milkshake,

As the waitress comes by,
she offers to take
a family photograph.
She holds up the camera,

and says, "Smile."

About the Author

Gina Marselle, M.A.Ed, resides in New Mexico with her husband and children. She has published poetic work with *The Sunday Poem Online Series,* in the *Alibi, the Rag, SIC3, Adobe Walls: An anthology of New Mexico poetry, Catching Calliope, Fix and Free Poetry Anthology I and II,* and *La Palabra Anthology I and II.* Marselle has one self-published chapbook titled *'Round Midnight* (2012).
She has coordinated the poetry event for the Summer Open Space Series sponsored by The City of Albuquerque since 2009.

Aside from poetry, she is an accomplished photographer. Her photos of New Mexico poets have been featured in the Santa Fe magazine *Trend* (March, 2011). She also photographed the cover of Jessica Helen Lopez' poetry book, *Always Messing With Them Boys* (West End Press, 2011), and has her photography featured in *September: traces of letting go* a poetry book by Katrina K Guarascio (Swimming With Elephants Publications, 2014).

A Fire of Prayer: A Collection of Poetry and Photography is her first full-length manuscript published by Swimming With Elephants Publications (2015).

How Photography Found Me

I went to Webster University in St. Louis, MO for professional training in acting. However, once at Webster, I soon found more interesting topics and study off stage. When I switched majors to Communication, I had to take a film class as a requirement. I took *Introduction to Photography*. I still have my notes that are yellowed with age and curled at the corners. My dad bought me a Vivitar 35mm SLR camera. Flash, lens, strap, camera bag, a few rolls of Fuji film, and the camera for fewer than 300 dollars.

I graduated with Honors from Webster University's School of Communication with an Emphasis in Photography. My expertise has always been 35mm SLR black and white photographs documenting life.

Fast forward many years later to this book, and the photos show this careful study of my art. All the photos were taken on my iPhone 4s throughout adventures with family or friends. All photos taken in color and edited for black and white in iPhoto. They are printed in color on the pages of this book. It is not the camera that takes any photo, it is the photographer, and my greatest tool is light and shadows.

~Gina

Photograph Acknowledgements

- Cover Art: Navy Pier Ferris Wheel, (original ferris wheel designed by George Washington Gale Ferris, Jr. as a landmark for the 1893 World's Columbian Exposition in Chicago), Chicago, Illinois.
- Page 8: Metal Structure, part of Albuquerque's Public Art Program, Tingley Beach, Albuquerque, New Mexico.
- Page 12: Navy Pier Ferris Wheel, Chicago, Illinois.
- Page 16: Parking Garage Elevator, 7th Floor, Chicago, Illinois.
- Page 24: Metal Structure, part of Albuquerque's Public Art Program, Tingley Beach, Albuquerque, New Mexico.
- Page 29: Detail of a Metal Structure, part of Albuquerque's Public Art Program, Tingley Beach, Albuquerque, New Mexico.
- Page 32: Self Portrait (look in the window), Secret Door to Vernon's Hidden Valley Steakhouse, Los Rancho de Albuquerque, New Mexico.
- Page 35: Metal Srtucture, part of Albuquerque's Public Art Program, Tingley Beach, Albuquerque, New Mexico.
- Page 41: Detail of Dan Namingha's Kachina "Symbolism I (1997)", Albuquerque Museum Outdoor Sculpture Garden, Albuquerque, New Mexico.
- Page 51: Union Station Train Stop City Scene from the Upper Level Outdoor Parking Lot, Kansas City, Missouri.
- Page 55: North Bridge Sidewalk Placard, Artist Unknown, Chicago, Illinois.
- Page 58: Author headshot taken at the National Hispanic Cultural Center, Albuquerque, NM, photo credit: Miranda Marselle.

Additional Acknowledgements

The author would like to acknowledge with sincere appreciation *The Sunday Poem* online series for publishing "Time Traveler" (August 2010) and "Ode to My Son" (April 2013). Thank you to *La Palabra: Mothers and Daughters* (Swimming With Elephants Publication) for publishing "Mīror" and "A Mother's Body" in their 2014 anthology. Also, thank you to the *Fixed and Free Anthology 2015* for pervious publication of the poem "tangerine."

Gratitude

Thank you to my husband, children, family and friends for always encouraging me. Thanks to my mom who helped me title the first poem I ever wrote when I was 17 (*Silent Flight*). Thanks to my dad who bought me my first camera in college. I also wish to thank poet, teacher, editor, and visionary, Katrina K Guarascio for always believing in my photography and poetry, and for publishing my first full-length manuscript.

Also available from
Swimming with Elephants Publications, LLC

Some of it is Muscle
Zachary Kluckman

Light as a Feather
An Anthology of Survival

September
Katrina K Guarascio & Gina Marselle

Heartbreak Ridge and Other Poems
Bill Nevins

Verbrennen
Matthew Brown

To Anyone Who has Ever Loved a Writer
Nika Ann

Of Small Children/ And Other Poor Swimmers
Brian Hendrickson

Find more publications and more information regarding Swimming with Elephants Publications at swimmingwithelephants.com

Copyright © 2015 Swimming with Elephants Publications

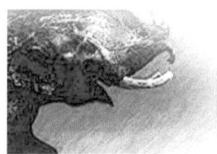

www.ingramcontent.com/pod-product-compliance
Lightning Source LLC
Chambersburg PA
CBHW041525090426
42736CB00035B/14